Surya

Indra

Ram

Hanuman

Soma

Yama

This book belongs to

....

....

....

Nita Mehta
Enriching Young Minds

TELL ME ABOUT
HINDU GODS & GODDESSES

Anurag Mehta

Vaneeta Vaid

Nita Mehta
Enriching Young Minds

TELL ME ABOUT HINDU GODS & GODDESSES

Reprint 2010

ISBN 978-81-7676-069-0

Illustrations: *Nita Mehta* Enriching Young Minds

Layout and laser typesetting:

National Information Technology Academy
3A/3, Asaf Ali Road
New Delhi-110002
☎ 23252948

Published by:

 Nita Mehta
Enriching Young Minds

3A/3 Asaf Ali Road, New Delhi-110002
Tel: 91-11-23250091, 29214011, 23252948, 29218727
Fax: 91-11-29225218, 91-11-23250091
E-Mail : nitamehta@nitamehta.com
Website : http://www.nitamehta.com

Contributing Writers:
Subhash Mehta
Tanya Mehta

Editorial & Proofreading:
Ekta
Deepali

Distributed by :
NITA MEHTA BOOKS
3A/3, Asaf Ali Road, New Delhi - 02
Distribution Centre:
D16/1, Okhla Industrial Area, Phase-I,
New Delhi-110020
Tel.: 26813199, 26813200

Price: Rs. 395/-

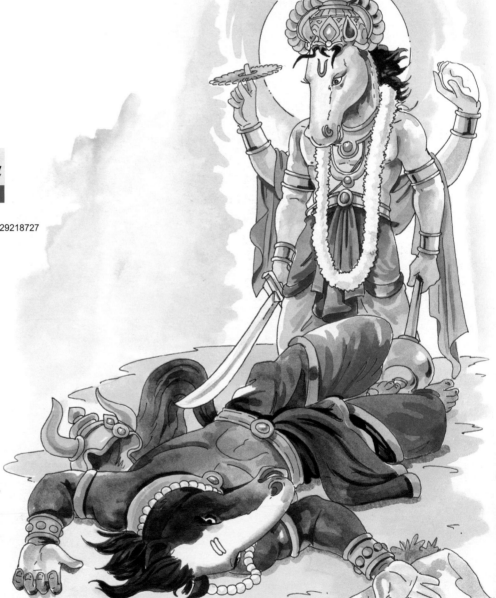

Contents

HINDU GODDESSES

Introduction

Our book Hindu Gods and Goddesses, tells us about the correlation of human mind, body, soul and environment divinity. Here we learn why Hanuman is compared to the human mind and Ganga to purity. Through these pages, we discover that Ganesha's broken tusk may just be linked to the waning and waxing of the moon! These events manifest as interesting tales that reflect our rich culture, as well as echo tales that are meant to familiarize children with our mythology. Keeping this in mind, the text helped by vivid illustrations, has been kept very simple.

God Made Himself

The earliest chronicles claim that Hindus believe that there is one God - The Supreme Being. No one created him. That means God created himself.

The Supreme Being is formless and omnipresent. What do you mean by omnipresent? It means that he is everywhere.

Hindus believe God is formless and omnipresent

On the other hand, Hinduism is often labeled as a religion having 330 million Gods. This concept leads to confusion if not understood properly.

Hindus believe in the presence of one God, the Supreme Being, but they believe him to have various aspects. Hindus have represented God in innumerable forms. All the Hindu Gods and Goddesses are various aspects of one God.

How Did it All Begin?

According to Hinduism, at first there was nothing. God was curious. He desired to know himself. He awakened and decided to send his representatives to create and evolve what we see today as our world and the universe. God is said to have initially created nature or **'prakriti'**.

Who were God's first representatives? These were **Lord Vishnu**, **Lord Brahma** and **Lord Shiva**. They were given the tasks of preservation, creation and destruction, respectively.

Lord Brahma

Lord Vishnu

In this context, destruction does not mean a negative activity. **Lord Shiva** would destroy the old to bring in the new; thus completing the cycle of existence.

Vishnu, **Brahma** and **Shiva** are the main Hindu Gods. Together, they form the **Trinity**.

Lord Shiva

Brahma-Vishnu-Shiva Appear for the First Time

How did Lord Brahma, Lord Vishnu and Lord Shiva appear? They all did not materialize just like that. In fact, amazing events unfolded before they appeared. It is said that at first there was nothing except for water and black spaces. Then came the serpent. A huge serpent with thousand heads. This coiled serpent, rode time for a million years. However, one moment of time, saw things alter in an unexpected and dramatic manner. What had happened? Over the pitch dark, water soaked lines, a golden light broke out for the first time!

A Golden Light Broke Out

The light shimmered and shone. As the light grew brighter, within the spaces, deep down underneath, a hum erupted which sounded like "Omm...!" As the hum reached its crescendo, so did the light above. Responding to these spectacular changes, the serpent loosened its coils. From within its coils, emerged someone. He was **Lord Vishnu**.

Lord Vishnu Awakens

Even as Lord Vishnu stood, a lotus flower began to blossom from his navel. The lotus grew out and landed on to the waters.

Within the lotus, sat **Lord Brahma**.

"Welcome, Brahma! The time for creation has come," Lord Vishnu smiled.

Brahma nodded sagely. Standing on the lotus, in a deep voice, Brahma began to chant the spells of creation.

A Lotus forms from Vishnu's navel

Lord Brahma appears

But he was rudely interrupted. Out of nowhere, sprang two demons called **Madhu** and **Kaitabha**.

A startled Brahma looked towards Vishnu for protection. Vishnu frowned at the demons. From his frown, emerged the figure of a fiery warrior, draped in skins, holding a trident (forked weapon).

Vishnu frowns at the demons

With one blow of his trident, the warrior finished the two demons. He was **Lord Shiva**. With the coming of Lord Shiva, the **Trinity** of the main Hindu Gods was complete.

Lord Shiva finishes the Demons

The Trinity...

What do you mean by the Trinity? Brahma-Vishnu-Shiva form the Trinity. The other name for Trinity is **Trimurti**. The Trinity are supposed to collectively represent God and carry out his orders. What is God's order? The smooth running of nature is the most important task assigned by God to the Trinity.

The Trinity is linked to Nature. Existence we all know is marshaled by the cycle of nature. Things are created, then they are preserved, and eventually they are destroyed to bring in the new. Observe how your morning begins and the day ends. First, the day is created. It is maintained and then it finally fades into night.

The point here is, the main Hindu Gods come together in a Trinity to smoothly set into motion, the wheels of the cycle of nature.

The Trinity represent the Cycle of Nature

How did Brahma create the world? Brahma firstly split the lotus, he had emerged from, into three parts. With one part of the lotus, he created the heavens, with the second part, he created the earth and with the third part, he created the skies. This way, he fashioned three worlds. He then shaped things to occupy these worlds, making sure that there was everything the earth and the universe needed to survive and grow.

"These worlds have to always abide by the rules and process of nature. They will always evolve (grow) through the paths of time," declared Brahma. This meant that the existence that Brahma was creating, was timeless and bound by the laws of nature or a life cycle.

Swarga

By the instructions of God, Brahma created three worlds.

SWARGA: The abode of the *Devas*. This is also called heaven and is situated above the earth.

BHU-LOKA: The abode of humans and all earthly beings. This is called earth. It is in the middle of Swarga and Patala.

PATALA: The abode of the *Asuras* (demons). This is a world below the earth or the underworld.

Above all these abodes is **SATYALOKA** or **BRAHMALOKA**, **VAIKUNTHA** and **KAILASA.** These are the abodes of Brahma, Vishnu and Shiva respectively.

Bhu-Loka

Patala

Brahma Appoints Devas

Brahma created, then appointed souls whom he called **'Devas'** or Gods, to take care of heaven and earth. They were called elements of nature. "These are your kingdoms," he announced to these elements.

"You shall provide heat to my creations. You shall travel through the skies making sure that every area receives heat," Brahma told **Surya**.

Surya, the sun-god, is orange hued and mounts a chariot drawn by seven red horses. Each horse is named for a day of the week.

Surya's Chariot of Seven Horses

Brahma cupped his palms and drew a flame of fire from Surya. He threw it towards the worlds saying, "You are **Agni** (fire), you have the powers to purify and consume. Your vehicle will be the ram (goat)."

Do you know why Agni's image shows him with a paunch (bulging stomach)? The paunch represents his ability to consume anything.

Agni's Paunch represents his ability to consume anything

"Lord **Indra**, you are the chief administrator of the heavens," Brahma uttered, bringing Indra into existence.

Besides being an administrator, Lord Indra is also the rainmaker, bearer of thunder and conductor of lightning and storms. His weapon is the **Vajra** or thunderbolt. Indra rides a white elephant called **Airavat.**

Indra's Weapon, the Vajra or Thunderbolt

Brahma then formed winds.

"**Vayu**, you are the God of the breath. You will have amazing speed. You will ride a deer and be known for your swiftness. You will aid in spreading seeds/pollen over the earth, so the growth of life continues," Brahma informed Lord Vayu after he had created him.

Vayu

Varuna riding Makara

Brahma raised his hands and filled spaces with gushing blue waters. Then he created Lord **Varuna**.

"Varuna, you are the God of the oceans." Brahma then sprinkled endless fish into the ocean saying, "Out of all these fish, you will ride a fish called **Makara**."

23

The Five Elements of Nature...

"All of you", Brahma addressed the five Devas he had created, "are the five most important elements of nature. If your rules are followed, there will remain a balance in existence forever."

After this, Lord Brahma filled the heavens with lesser gods or **Devas**, who would be the assistants for his appointed elements.

When Lord Brahma finished his job of formation, Lord Vishnu took on the task of preserving whatever Brahma had formed. On the other hand, Lord Shiva watched creation and preservation, then came forth to whittle away anything, which grew out of the range of maintenance (preservation) and had faded out. He destroyed and removed it, so Brahma could re-create it.

Devas Become Asuras...

Alas! Some of the lesser Devas were stricken with the disease of greed. They were not satisfied with just one part of heavens or the wealth of natural resources, which went with them to earth. They wanted more. Now greed can really change everything. Not only did the insides of these Gods turn their spirit dark with wickedness, but their bodies sprouted evil sores and ugly horns. These demonic Devas began to unsettle the working of the heavens. Furious, the other Gods pushed them off the limits of heaven. These fallen Gods dashed under the earth to create their own kingdoms, which became **Patal Lok** or the underworlds. They became *Asuras* or demons, the timeless enemies of all Hindu Gods.

Demons being pushed off the heavens

Goddesses

The Trinity and other Gods had their own consorts or wives. The consorts or wives of the Gods are called Goddesses. Hindu Goddess is called **Shakti** or strength of the world. She takes varied forms to help vanquish evil and rid the world of turmoil. Sometimes, she even becomes a warrior, to aid her husband or son to battle forces of evil.

Saraswati

Lakshmi

Brahma is married to Goddess **Saraswati**. She is the Goddess of *Wisdom* and *Science*, the mother of the *Vedas*. Vishnu's wife is **Lakshmi**, the Goddess of *Wealth*, who bestows blessings of *Harmony* and *Good life*.

Shiva's spouse **Parvati**, is the Goddess of *Peace*. She is supposed to take on many forms to sustain peace in the world. That means, Goddesses fought demons too! Goddess **Durga** was created to defeat the buffalo demon *Mahisha*. And Goddess **Kali** was created by Durga to defeat the demons *Chandra* and *Mundra*. Kali is considered to be the female version of Shiva as a destroyer.

Parvati

Kali

Humans on Earth

Legends say that after Saraswati and Brahma got married, they had a son called **Manu**. Manu was sent to earth as the first human! Manu got married to **Ananti** and they started the human race of which you and I are a part of!

Jiva Atma...

Brahma blessed creatures with their most important gift: he instilled *Jiva* or life within each body. Within each **Jiva**, he instilled an *atma* or soul too; therefore, **Jiva Atma** is in all living beings. It is the consciousness in all life forms.

Do you know what *consciousness* means?

It means being aware of one's surroundings. Any form instilled with **Jiva Atma** is aware of its environment, can feel pain, fear or death and wants to survive in the world of the living. The **Jiva Atma** also encourages the consciousness of humans to seek a meaning in life. All **Jivas** are spread across the three worlds. These worlds are all located beneath the abode or home of Lord Brahma, *Satya loka* or the place of truth.

Om

Remember, it was written that when the first divine light shone, a hum erupted too. That hum sounded like 'OMMMM'.

'Om' portrays the Hindu concept of the Supreme Being. It is believed that even all the Gods and Goddesses are venerated by this simple sound. 'Om' is considered to be the first sound that emerged when the creation of the worlds began. This symbol represents the whole universe in Hinduism.

The Planets are Also Gods

Some planets are also considered as Gods. There are nine planet Gods also referred to as *Navagrahas*; **Nava** (nine) **Grahas** (planets). These **Grahas** have a very important role in shaping fate or destinies of human beings. The placing of these planets is said to directly influence fate and change a person's existence. So the **Grahas** are considered to be very important.

The study of these planets to foretell the future is called **Astrology**. The **Sun**, **Moon**, **Mars**, **Mercury**, **Jupiter**, **Venus** and **Saturn**, along with the two lunar nodes, the North and South nodes, **Rahu** and **Ketu** are the **Navagrahas**.

Sun or Surya is a living God, whom everyone can see and pray to. He is the life-giver and according to the *Vedas* he is a witness to all actions.

Angaraka or **Mars** is regarded as a God of martial character, red in every aspect. **Brihaspati** or **Jupiter** is revered as the *Guru* of *devas*, and protector of the world.

Buddha or **Mercury** is considered as the greatest among the wise. This God bestows wisdom and wealth.

Chandra or Moon is a lovable and loving God. Sages and devotees invoke the Goddess Mother (radiating *amrit* to strengthen the mind) in **Chandra** and meditate for hours.

Shani or Saturn is a protector that may turn destroyer if angry.

Shukra or Venus is the bestower of long life, wealth, happiness, children, property and good education. He is the *Guru* of *asuras*. A beneficial God, he blesses the devotees with power to control one's *indriyas* (sense organs) and enables the devotees to obtain fame and name.

Lunar and Solar eclipses are said to occur because of **Rahu** and **Ketu**. There is an interesting story behind this.

Vishnu as Mohini strikes Rahu

The Story of Rahu and Ketu...

The **Devas** and the **Asuras** churned the ocean for the jar of *Amrit*. But as soon as it appeared, both the **Devas** and the **Asuras** started fighting over who would drink it.

Suddenly, Lord Vishnu, disguised himself as a beautiful maiden named **Mohini** and appeared before them. Mohini distracted the Asuras with her charm while she poured the *Amrit* down the throat of the Devas.

An Asura named Rahu, noticed this and changed himself into a Deva to drink the Amrit. But, as the Asura was about to have the *Amrit*, Surya, the Sun God and Chandra, the Moon God, cried out, "Stop! That's Rahu, the Asura."

The next moment, Vishnu's divine weapon, the **Chakra**, appeared in Mohini's hands. Before the *Amrit* could pass through Rahu's throat, the Chakra cut off his head. But some drops of the *Amrit* had been swallowed by the demon. Therefore, his body and severed head became immortal or undying.

This *immortal head* of the Asura is called '**Rahu**' and the *body* is called '**Ketu**'.

It is believed that this immortal head and body occasionally swallow the sun and the moon, causing Solar and Lunar Eclipses. Then the sun and the moon pass through the opening at the neck, ending the eclipse.

Why do Rahu and Ketu swallow the moon or the sun?

Because the sun and the moon were the ones who pointed out to Vishnu that Rahu was an Asura in disguise.

Rahu swallowing the Sun

Why so Many Gods?

"There is divinity (God) in everyone and everything," says Hinduism. How many Gods and Goddesses does Hinduism have? The figure 330 million is sometimes quoted, so is the figure one. And strange as it may seem, both are right. Hinduism recognizes that many people need a God they can feel close to; a God they can picture in their minds and worship. For a Hindu, God is ONE; we may call him by any name.

We pray to the representations of God, which has taken the shape of either a human, an animal or even trees and rivers. That is why Hinduism has so many Gods.

There are tree Gods, river Goddesses, sky Gods, animal Gods. Each has different powers to bless the world.

God is represented Everywhere

Animal Gods

Animal Gods occupy an important place in Hinduism. The main Hindu animal God is **Ganesha**, the son of Shiva and Parvati. He has the head of an elephant and the body of a human. This Elephant God is supposed to bring fortune and good luck to any one he blesses.

Hanuman, the Monkey God, son of the Wind God, is revered too. He is worshipped as the protector of mankind.

The '*Hanuman Chalisa*' (verses in praise Of Hanuman) is recited with prompt veneration in times of fear and anxiety.

Ganesha

Hanuman

Vehicles of Gods

These deities are revered too because some of them happen to be the transport of the Gods.

Each Hindu God has a personal vehicle for travelling. Vishnu sits on a **serpent**.

Shiva rides the **Nandi** bull. His wife Parvati, rides on a **Lion**. His son Ganesha rides a **Mouse**.

Shiva rides Nandi

Parvati rides a Lion

Ganesha rides a mouse

Airavat, the God of elephants, is Lord Indra's mode for traveling.

Garuda, the other vehicle of Vishnu, is a bird deity. Garuda's son is **Jatayu**, who tried to rescue Sita, when Ravana was fleeing after kidnaping her.

Garuda, the vehicle of Vishnu

Brahma rides a **swan**.

Kamdhenu, is the sacred cow deity.

Shesh Naag is the serpent God. He is considered to be the king of *Patala* or the underworld.

Brahma rides a swan.

Some other Vehicles of the Gods...

Ram (Agni)

Swan (Brahma)

Lion (Durga)

Mouse (Ganesha)

Elephant (Indra)

Peacock (Kartikeya)

Owl (Lakshmi)

Bull (Maheshwari)

Swan or Peacock (Saraswati)

Nandi-the bull (Shiva)

Seven Horses (Surya)

Seven Swans (Varuna)

Male Buffalo (Yama)

Elephant (Vishwakarma)

Thousand Horses (Vayu)

38

Knowledge

How do we know all this? It is said that Lord Vishnu breathed the truth to Brahma about the reality of existence. Brahma in turn told his celestial companions, who carried the stories to the first souls who came to be known as **Rishis** and **Sadhus** (saints). The rishis grasped the knowledge through the vibrations of *mantras*.

This knowledge is referred to as the **Vedas**. The saints or the rishis memorized the Vedas and passed them on to further generations. Not a single word was written and the Vedas had to be learned by heart.

Rishis Memorizing the Vedas

These **unwritten Vedas** are called as 'Shruti' scriptures. 'Shruti' means heard, experienced and spiritually revealed.

Later, the Vedas were compiled and put on paper. They were written in the Sanskrit language. The **written Vedas** are called 'Smriti' scriptures. As years went by, there were many additions to the Vedas. The Vedas form the basis of the faith we call Hinduism.

Smriti Scriptures

No Devil...

Hinduism does not have a Devil like it has an omnipresent God. There is no Overlord of the Asuras.

In Hinduism, right and wrong is defined by godliness or ungodliness. Evil is being ungodly. In fact the Asuras themselves pray to God for favours! Asuras, however, are never finished off the face of the earth; they are only put in their places. This way, they become examples in the fight between good and evil where good always triumphs.

Hindu Gods

Lord Brahma

It is said that Lord Brahma was the God appointed to create everything in the universe, including our world and all the living and non-living things residing within. As creation is the work of the mind and the intellect, Lord Brahma symbolizes the **Universal Mind**. He is the God who powers the mind to think creatively.

Brahma is married to Goddess Saraswati. She is the Goddess of wisdom and science, the mother of the Vedas and the inventor of the **Devanagari** script.

Lord Brahma Symbolizes the Universal Mind

Brahma is usually represented as a bearded, four-faced, four-armed, red-coloured deity. He carries a rosary in the upper right hand, a book in the upper left hand, a kamandal (water pot) in the lower left hand and bestows grace with his lower right hand. The four faces represent the sacred knowledge of the four Vedas (**Rig**, **Yajur**, **Sama**, and **Atharva**) which say that Brahma is the source of all information essential for the formation of the universe. The four arms represent the four directions declaring all encompassing presence of Lord Brahma. Brahma does not have a weapon, in this regard he is different from the other Gods.

Lord Brahma has no weapons

Symbols of Brahma...

Brahma rides the swan. The swan has a unique ability of making the correct choice. It is claimed that the swan can sniff out pure milk even if it is mixed with water! Similarly, Brahma riding this vehicle conveys the message that Brahma too has this quality where he too can choose and differentiate between every aspect of existence.

- If you observe the image of Brahma, he holds beads or a **rosary** in his back right hand. Now what does this rosary signify? The rosary denotes the time cycle through which the world moves from creation to maintenance, from sustenance to dissolution, and from dissolution to new creation.

- The **open front right hand** shows that the Lord imparts grace and protects all genuine devotees.

- Do you know why Brahma **wears off-white clothes**? Since pure white means purity, his off white clothes represents the acceptance of opposites in existence. For example: purity and impurity, happiness and unhappiness, vice and virtue, knowledge and ignorance.

- The **kamandal** (water pot) in the front left hand stands for the cosmic energy by which Brahma brings the universe into existence.

- What does the **book** in his hand mean? The book signifies that right knowledge is important for any kind of creative work.

- Brahma's face shines in a **golden tone** to show he is active. This also conveys the intensity with which Brahma performs his responsibilities of creation. His white beard represents ageless wisdom, while the length of the **beard** denotes the idea that creation is an ongoing procedure.

- The **crown** on Brahma's head indicates authority, which means he is in total control over the course of creation.

- Brahma sitting or standing on a **lotus** specifies that he embodies the creative power of the Trinity.

Brahma Lies to Shiva...

Long ago, there was a moment when Brahma, the creator and Vishnu, the preserver, got into a loud argument.

"It is I who is superior," stormed Lord Brahma, floating on his swan in the skies. Lord Vishnu laughed and dismissed this claim, "You know, it is not true. It is I who is the superior one between you and me."

The heated argument was so fierce that the celestial kingdom of the Gods shook with this war of words!

Shiva as an endless column of fire

The other Gods were worried and went to Lord Shiva, the destroyer. "They are quarrelling about who is superior of the two. Please do something," they begged Shiva.

Assuming the form of an unending column of fire, Shiva appeared in the middle of the conflicting duo. Brahma and Vishnu were taken aback, as they didn't realise what had come between them.

Ketaki lies

"The one who finds the beginning and the end of this column shall be declared superior," came instructions from the fiery, swaying, brilliant pillar of light. The two disputing Gods looked up the pillar of fire, but there was no top visible. They looked down and there was no bottom.

They decided to take the challenge. Brahma flew upwards on his swan tracing the top of the column. Vishnu went into the earth tracking the end of the column. Thousands of miles and many years of travel later, both the Gods were unsuccessful in their pursuit. During his futile search, Brahma came across a **Ketaki** flower.

"I was at the top. Someone had laid me as an offering! I have fallen down," **Ketaki** blinked. Picking up **Ketaki**, Brahma looked up but there was no top and he knew she was lying. But he decided to tell a small white lie himself! Returning, Brahma heard Vishnu confessing that he had not found the end of the column.

Shiva is Furious

"I have," announced Brahma. "This is **Ketaki**. She is my witness."

Oh no, Brahma had let ego guide his decision.

An Enraged Shiva caught his lie. Manifesting himself back to his true form, he admonished Brahma. Feeling very embarrassed, Brahma admitted that he had lied.

"No one shall pray to you. No one will offer Ketaki as a flower to the Gods. She lied and gave a false testimony," Shiva declared.

Hence, it is not surprising that there are no temples for Brahma except for one in Rajasthan. Yet in all Shiva and Vishnu temples, there is an image of Lord Brahma on the Northern wall and he is considered to be one of the important deities.

Brahma image

Brahma creates Saraswati

When Brahma Created Saraswati…

Amongst his many creations, Brahma also created a woman. This woman, came to be known by different names: **Satarupa**, **Saraswati**, **Sandhya** or **Brahmi.**

Brahma was so enraptured by his own creation that he fell in love with her. His gaze could not leave her. Embarrassed by this, to avoid his gaze, she moved to his left, then behind him, and then to his right. But a head sprang up wherever she shifted. Brahma was able to see her from every angle because he created a head anywhere she moved! Nervously, the lady sprang up in the air.

51

Alas! A fifth head displayed itself on top of Brahma's four heads. Brahma then asked her to marry him and help him create the universe. He lived with her for a hundred years, at the end of which, Manu was born.

Brahma Sprouts Heads to see Saraswati

Now Only Four Heads...

There are different explanations for Brahma having only four heads now and not five. One myth declares that this is so because during the argument between Vishnu and Brahma on the 'Who is superior?' issue, Brahma spoke very rudely to Shiva. In anger, Shiva cut one of Brahma's heads off!

Lord Vishnu

The next God in the Trinity is Lord Vishnu. Gracious and handsome, this God reclines on a thousand headed serpent called Shesh Naag. The serpent spreads its hood in a protective cover over Vishnu as he floats in the heavens.

Vishnu is the **Lord of Protection**, provision and maintenance. Vishnu's spouse is Lakshmi, the Goddess of wealth. Vishnu and Lakshmi assist Jiva Atmas that are established into existence by Brahma, to continue the cycle of life.

Lord Vishnu is mostly shown with a human body having four arms.

Symbols of Vishnu...

- In his hands, Vishnu carries a conch (**shankha**), a mace (**gada**), and a discus (**chakra**).

- Vishnu's four arms mean that he is omnipresent and all-powerful.

- He blows a conch to remind everyone to live in this world with kindness and compassion towards all living beings.

- The **chakra** in his upper right hand is his weapon. This is to show that Vishnu uses this weapon to protect his followers from evil.

- The mace shows energy within Vishnu. Vishnu needs this energy to maintain the world.

- His open palmed lower right hand shows him showering blessings on his devotees.

- Why does Vishnu ride a snake? The snake represents all the desires found in existence. By riding the snake, Vishnu shows he controls all the desires that exist.

- Vishnu floats over blue skies. The colour blue depict the sign of infinity or endlessness. This suggests that Vishnu lights up the entire universe.

- Vishnu's body is also blue, signifying that like the skies he too is formless, and immeasurable.

- Yellow is the colour of earth. His yellow clothes means that he incarnates himself on this earth to uphold righteousness and to destroy evil.

Chakra

Conch Shell

Mace

Vishnu Comes to Earth...

Lord Vishnu is the God who comes to earth in different guises (appearances). Now why would he do that? For the simple reason of helping humanity to fight trouble makers. Trouble makers are *Asuras* and any other ungodly beings who prefer the paths of extreme wickedness. To put them in their place, Vishnu comes to earth. He is called an *Avatar* or hero who comes to save people from adversity.

Vishnu's Nine Avatars

Matsaya

Kurma

How many times did Lord Vishnu come to earth? Lord Vishnu has come to earth nine times. His nine incarnations are also seen as stages of evolution for mankind. His various forms or *Avatars* were: **Matsaya** (fish), **Kurma** (tortoise), **Varaha** (boar), **Narasimha** (man-lion), **Vamana** (dwarf), **Parashurama** (a powerful warrior), **Ram**, **Krishna**, **Buddha**.

Predictions say that his tenth *Avatar* **Kalki** (machine-man) will come at the end of the present age (**Kaliyuga**). Kalki will come riding a white horse.

Varaha

Narasimha

Vamana

Parashurama

Krishna

Ram

Buddha

Lord Ram...

Lord Vishnu reincarnated as Ram and came to earth to help the troubled people. Ram was born as the prince of Ayodhya and represented all that was good in the world. Ram became very popular and is worshipped in this *Avatar* of Vishnu even today. Ram's most devoted companion was Hanuman, the Monkey God.

Lord Ram

Lord Krishna...

Once again, Vishnu was born on earth to help the unhappy public. This time, he was born as **Krishna**. Lord Krishna defeated the evil king **Kansa** and brought peace to the lands.

Krishna spoke of duty and **Karma**. His words are written in the holy book called the **Bhagvad Gita**. Like Lord Ram, Lord Krishna too became very popular and is worshipped even today.

Lord Krishna

Lord Vishnu usually comes to the rescue of the Devas and his disciples. In fact, many a times, Lord Brahma himself needs to send his disciples to Vishnu for help. Here is an interesting tale when Brahma did just that.

The Horse Headed Asura...

"I want to be immortal," **Hayagriva**, the horse headed *Asura*, requested Brahma.

"That is not possible," Brahma sagely shook his head as he reclined on his celestial seat.

Hayagriva requesting Brahma

"Then please allow me this boon," Hayagriva uttered plaintively, "allow me to be killed only by the one, who also has a horse-head like me."

Brahma unthinkingly granted the boon. What Brahma did not realize that Hayagriva was one of a kind. There was no one like him, in the entire cosmos! Thus, he believed that he could not be killed. Naturally, undeterred, Hayagriva created havoc everywhere. In fact, with evil intent, Hayagriva stole one Veda from Brahma too. Desperately, the Devas rushed to Lord Brahma for help.

"Ask Lord Vishnu. He will surely help you," advised Lord Brahma.

Termites eating the Bow

When the Devas reached, they saw Lord Vishnu in a deep slumber. Vishnu was sleeping with his head resting over his bow. In the spur of the moment, the Devas devised a plan.

As planned, they sent termites to powder the bow. Oh dear, as soon as the wood of the bow was eaten, the bowstring broke so hard that the pressure sliced Vishnu's neck too!

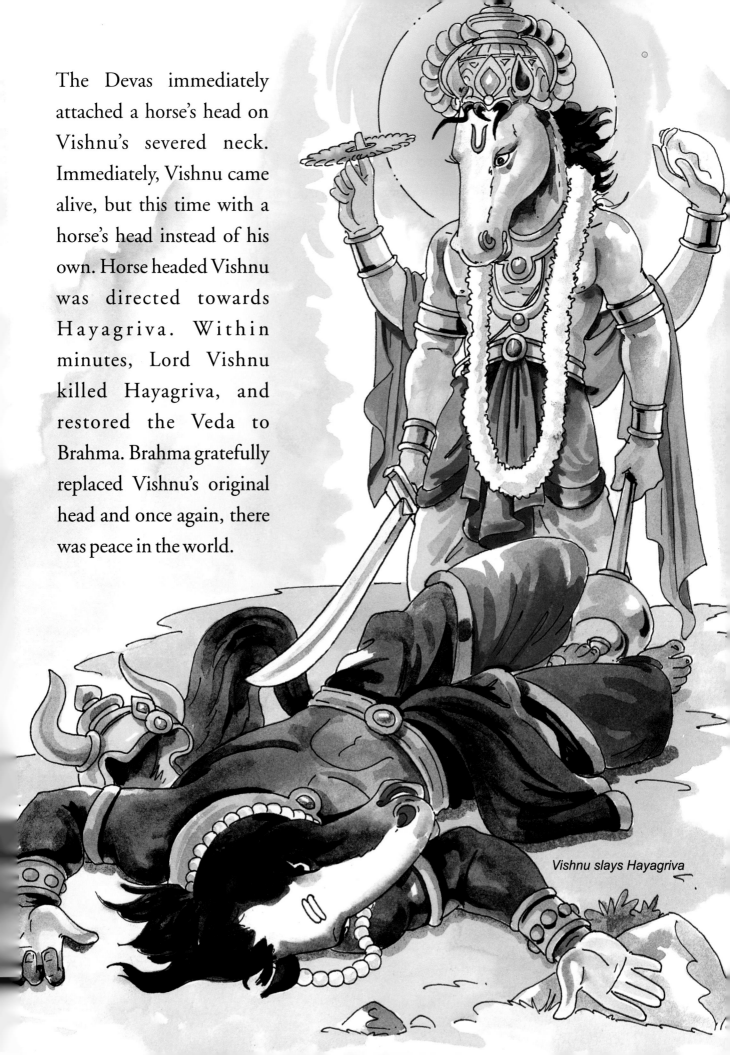

The Devas immediately attached a horse's head on Vishnu's severed neck. Immediately, Vishnu came alive, but this time with a horse's head instead of his own. Horse headed Vishnu was directed towards Hayagriva. Within minutes, Lord Vishnu killed Hayagriva, and restored the Veda to Brahma. Brahma gratefully replaced Vishnu's original head and once again, there was peace in the world.

Vishnu slays Hayagriva

Lord Shiva

Shiva is known as the **Lord of Destruction**. He is important because he destroys everything, so the new can be born or recreated. He is also called *Mahayogi,* or the great ascetic, who meditates with austere concentration on high mountain ranges.

Lord Shiva and his family

Shiva has 1,008 names. It is believed that Shiva, along with his wife Parvati and two sons, **Ganesha** and **Kartekeya**, live on Mount Kailash, in the Himalayas. What transport does Shiva use? He uses Nandi, the bull. Shiva guards himself with a trident or *Trishul*. Shiva is represented in human form but is dressed only in skins and covered with ashes and has a blue throat.

Why does Shiva have a Blue Throat ?...

The story dates back to a million years. The Asuras and the Devas were tasked by Vishnu to churn the ocean of milk, which was in the heavens. Now why would Vishnu ask them to do that ? It all started with the holy sage Durvasa cursing Indra. With much indulgence, Durvasa had presented Indra with a garland.

"Bless you and may all your troubles cease," Durvasa had said, handing Indra the garland. Indra, instead of politely receiving the garland, hung it on his elephant's tusk. Durvasa was livid and he declared that Indra as well as all the other Devas would lose their powers, become weak and then die.

Ridden with anxiety from this curse, Indra and the other Gods approached Vishnu for help.

"Churn the ocean. It is a tough task so enlist the help of the Asuras also. At the bottom of the ocean, lies the nectar of health and immortality. Once you drink that, you will never grow weak. His orders were complied. But during the process, a disaster struck. As the ocean was being churned, an urn full of poisonous gases popped up.

Urn full of poisonous gases

This sent everyone into a dizzy faint. Shiva, who was sitting on Mount Kailash, saw this. Within seconds, he reached the scene, grasped the toxic urn and swallowed the poison.

Shiva, however, underestimated the potency of the poison. The poison tore down his throat making it blue. Seeing this, Goddess Shakti, immediately shafted an arrow into Shiva's neckline; controlling the poison from spreading further. Shiva fell down. Holding his throat, Shiva writhed in pain. Moon God, at once, slanted his cooling rays over Shiva's throat and Shiva felt better. However, his throat remained blue. He was called *Neel Kantha* or the blue throated one, after this incident.

Know Shiva...

- Another image of Shiva is the **Shivalinga**. The Shivalinga represents that column of fire which Shiva represented when the argument over 'Who is Superior?' issue took place between Vishnu and Brahma .

- Lord Shiva is called the Master of Yoga.

- Shiva wears a snake, **Vasuki** around his neck. Vasuki Naga is shown curled three times around the neck of the Lord and is looking towards his right side. The snake shows that God's eternal laws of reason and justice preserve natural order in the universe.

- The **three coils of the snake** symbolize the past, present and future – time in cycles.

- He is also known as **Neel Kantha** (blue-throated), for he holds Vasuki's poison in his throat.

- **Rudra** is another name of Shiva. Rudra also means 'strict or uncompromising' and **aksha** means eye. The '*Rudraksha*' necklace worn by the Lord demonstrates that he uses his cosmic or heavenly laws firmly, without compromise, to maintain law and order in the universe. The necklace has 108 beads which represent the elements used in the creation of the world.

- A **crescent moon** adorns his forehead, suggesting his control on the time cycle.

- Shiva is also called **Pashupatinath** or Lord of the Animals. Shiva sits on a tiger skin declaring his control over the savage wild life.

- A **third eye** on his forehead, shows Shiva as the source of knowledge and wisdom.

- The pure and pristine **Ganga** trapped in Shiva's locks signifies that the Lord destroys sin, removes ignorance, and bestows knowledge, purity and peace on the devotees.

- The **damru** or small drum shows Shiva's involvement in creative activity too.

Shiva and Dance...

Shiva created dance. He is supposed to have
created the first 16 rhythmic syllables ever
pronounced in the Sanskrit language. Shiva has
many forms of dance of which his dance of anger is called
the Raudra Tandava and his dance of joy, the
Ananda Tandava.

In Tamil Nadu, the great temple of Chidambaram
was built, the only one in India dedicated to Shiva as
Nataraja, the Lord of Dance. Lord Shiva is also the
Lord of Mercy and Compassion. He protects
devotees from evil forces such as lust, greed, and anger.
He grants boons, bestows grace and awakens
wisdom in his devotees.

Hanuman-The Monkey God

Hanuman is the Hindu Monkey God. He is the son of the God of Wind, **Vayu** and the heavenly fairy, **Anjana**.

Dashratha accepts Kheer from Agni

Anjana was once a celestial maiden but she was born on earth as a monkey woman as a result of a curse. When the king of Ayodhya, **Dashratha**, performed a *yagna* praying for a son; he was given a bowl of *kheer* by the fire God, Agni. **Dashratha's** wives shared the *kheer* amongst themselves and thus four sons were born to them.

Kheer falling into Anjana's hands

A portion of this *kheer* was carried away by the Lord of wind, Vayu, and fell in the hands of Anjana. Thus, Anjana gave birth to Hanuman. That is why Hanuman is also known as *Pavanputra* or the son of Vayu.

Hanuman grew up to be a strong and mischievous monkey boy. He had powers that enabled him to fly. He could travel anywhere within seconds. Do you know, once, as a child, Hanuman mistook the sun to be a fruit! When he reached out to snatch what he thought was a fruit, Lord Indra was so upset that he struck Hanuman with his thunderbolt.

Young Hanuman leaps for the Sun

Distressed at seeing his son being attacked, Lord Vayu angrily decided not to provide vital air to the worlds. This created chaos and an uproar in the worlds. Begging for forgiveness, all the Gods offered to bestow boons on Hanuman as an appeasement. This pleased Vayu and he relented. With the boons, Hanuman became so powerful that he was invincible. He could fly with great speed, he could shrink and expand, he developed immense strength, agility and intelligence.

Rishi cursing Little Hanuman

But, as Hanuman grew up, there was no one who could challenge him. His naughty deeds increased and he loved to tease the rishis. Their pompous reactions to his teasing delighted young Hanuman enormously!

The rishis were not pleased at all. In fact, they were irritated. Hanuman was having so much of fun that he really did not care. This continued teasing culminated into one big curse from the rishis, "You will forget that you have these powers. You will only come to know of it when someone reminds you ."

This had an electric effect on Hanuman. He was immediately subdued. Hanuman moved on to educate himself by learning the scriptures from Lord Surya. Hanuman became so scholarly that he came to be regarded as the body of knowledge. He had no memory of his powers to fly, to expand and shrink at will or anything else. He became an ocean of virtues and a friend of the pure hearted.

It was years later when he joined Lord Ram, (the reincarnation of Vishnu, who came to earth to battle evil), that Hanuman remembered his powers. Hanuman eventually played an important part in the war between good and evil, that is the war between Ram and Ravan. Hanuman also became an ardent devotee of Lord Ram. In the modern era too, the picture of Hanuman, as a humble devotee of Lord Ram, is very popular.

Hanuman is the devotee of Lord Ram

Hanuman in different images...

Bhakta Hanuman:

Hanuman is seen holding both hands together in prayer.

Bhakta Hanuman

Veer Hanuman:

He holds a mace in one hand and a mountain in the other.

Veer Hanuman

Did you know the Human Mind is Compared to Hanuman?...

Why are the qualities of Hanuman compared to the human mind? This is said because the mind is fickle (like a monkey) and leaps here and there at will.

Hanuman is compared to the Human Mind

The mind, like Hanuman can also travel where it wants to, within seconds. The mind can also expand or shrink itself anytime (again like Hanuman). The control of the mind is important otherwise there will be tension and stress.

If the mind remains unstable it causes problems and disturbances. This again points to the time young Hanuman teased the rishis. It is recommended that one should concentrate in cleansing the mind with thoughts of God,(as did Hanuman in his devotion to Lord Ram). Once your mind is stable, your intelligence can perform highly.

Lord Ganesha

"The first being you find facing the North direction, bring his head to me," Lord Shiva ordered his soldiers.

Now why did Lord Shiva need a head?

The legend goes that once in a fit of anger, Shiva cut off the head of a boy his wife had created. Parvati had given the boy, the breath of life and had adopted him as her son. She was inconsolable when Shiva unknowingly cut his head off.

The soldiers bring an Elephant Head

The boy was guarding their home entrance, at Parvati's request, when the horrible incident happened. Not recognizing him, (since Parvati had made the boy in Shiva's absence), Shiva challenged the boy; asking him to move aside so Shiva could enter. Now the boy did not recognize Shiva at all! So he refused to let him enter. This culminated into a heated exchange, which led to the drastic act by Shiva.

Shiva fixes the head on the boy's Neck

Parvati was inconsolable when she found her adopted son, lying lifeless and beheaded on the ground. Extremely apologetic of his thoughtless act Shiva wanted to make amends. That is why he sent his soldiers to fetch a head. The soldiers quickly delivered the head of the first being they came across facing North (the North direction is associated with wisdom). It was the head of an elephant. With quick execution Shiva fitted the elephant head on to the boy's inert neck. Moving a little away, Shiva chanted *mantras*. The elephant-headed boy came alive!

Ganesha lives with Shiva , Parvati and his brother Kartekeya at Mount Kailash. There are many tales told about Ganesha's childhood. Like any child, his anecdotes want to make you laugh. But Ganesha hated being laughed at. In fact, once the moon laughed at Ganesha and he really had to regret it!

The Moon Teases Ganesha…

"Aha, today is my birthday and I shall eat lots of *laddoos*," Ganesha slurped to his rat.

"Let's go! A devotee has invited me to his house for a feast."

Ganesha was extremely happy when he saw the pile of *laddoos* set before him at the devotees home.

"Munch-yum-munch munch, munch!"

Ganesha eating the Laddoos

Ganesha eagerly picked off the laddoos with his trunk from the plate. He ate and ate till his belly began to swell. "Burp!" went Ganesha and his belly shook!

"Now, I am satisfied. I have eaten so many laddoos that I can hardly move. Rat, take me home."

Ganesha mounted his rat and left.

The rat with Ganesha on his back weaved through paths. Suddenly, a snake abruptly came in their way. The rat skidded and in doing so, he threw Ganesha off.

"Bump!"

Ganesha rolled and with a thump, his stomach burst open.

"Plonk- plonk- plonk!"

Laddoos spilled from his tummy. Horrified, Ganesha looked around; his trunk curling with acute embarrassment. He was sure no one was around to see his ridiculous situation.

"Wait rat, let me put the *laddoos* back into my stomach," Ganesha uttered. Quickly filling his stomach again, Ganesha realized that the *laddoos* kept spilling out from his open belly.

"Aha, I have an idea," Ganesha muttered, glancing at the slinking snake.

"Whup!"

Ganesha falls and his stomach bursts open

Ganesha seized the snake and said,

"Sorry snake, I am going to use you as a belt to hold my tummy full of laddoos."

He then tightened the 'snake belt' and held back all the *laddoos* into his big belly.

"Let's go," Ganesha instructed his ride.

Just as Ganesha remounted his vehicle, he heard a chuckle.

Ganesh uses the snake as a belt

"Who is that?" Ganesha curiously flapped his ears and looked around. There was no one on the surface.

"Ha, ha, ha, so funny! Ha, ha, using a snake belt...*laddoos* spilling, heee heee!"

Again someone giggled.

The Moon giggles

Now Ganesha was extremely angry. Who was mocking him? He looked up and saw the culprit. It was the moon. The moon was giggling helplessly at the sight of Ganesha and his stomach full of laddoos tied with a snake.

Now this made Ganesha really angry. He went crimson.

"How dare you laugh at me."

But the moon was quite taken in by the funny sight and kept up his mirth.

Ganesha was so angry that he broke a part of his tusk and hurled it at the moon, saying piercingly,

"I curse you! You will never shine at night from now."

Ganesha curses the moon

Till then, the moon used to shine every night. Just as soon as Ganesha said that, the moon disappeared and the sky went inky black. Ganesha rode off, fuming.

"Aieeee, where is the moon?" people on the earth frantically asked.

"Where is the moon?" said the Gods in heaven too.

Nights became miserable for the earth and heaven. Gloomy darkness besieged them every evening.

"This is Ganesha's doing. He is angry with the moon for laughing at him. Let's go and beg Ganesha to forgive the moon," suggested someone.

So people as well as the Gods went to Ganesha.

"Please bring the moon back. Please forgive it for laughing," chorused everyone. Now Ganesha was not the one to carry grudges.

"Hmmm, I will bring the moon back."

Everyone clapped happily at this.

"But on one condition," declared Ganesha, still a little miffed at the moon's audacity.

"What condition?" queried all.

"Henceforth, the moon is sentenced to wax and wane. It will alternate between a shining fortnight and a dark fortnight. Each period will end by a full moon and a new moon."

"Oh, thank you," everyone bowed.

A waxing and waning moon was better than no moon, you see.

Did you know that till today, people consider it inauspicious to look at the moon on *Ganesha Chaturthi*. That is Ganesha's birthday and the day the moon dared to laugh at him.

The portrayal of Lord Ganesha as a blend of human and animal parts symbolizes the ideals of perfection and spiritual significance.

- The **large elephant head** of Ganesha symbolizes wisdom and understanding.

- An elephant trunk is strong yet gentle too. This means that you need strength to face the rigours of the outside world, yet you also need gentleness to handle your inner self. If you notice **Ganesha's trunk**, it is coiled like an 'OM'. OM is the first word or sound that erupted at the beginning of the world and it is supposed to hold in its single word, venerations to all Hindu Gods and Goddesses.

- The large **ears** of Ganesha signify great listening powers. To be able to listen to everything without distraction means that one can carefully collect ideas and reach perfection in all ventures.

- Ganesha has two **tusks** which indicate wisdom and emotion. His left tusk is broken. Many legends give a reason for the broken left tusk. It is claimed that Ganesha broke the tusk in a war with a demon. One of the more popular lore's say that he broke it when the moon teased him.

- Ganesha's **elephant eyes** sees things larger than they really are. Thus encouraging the message of respect towards your fellow beings. How is that? When one sees others to be bigger than oneself, automatically, one feels humbled and respect follows naturally.

- Ganesha's **four arms** indicate the aura of a being who is omnipresent.

- A tray of **laddoos** (sweets) near the Lord denotes that he bestows wealth and prosperity upon his devotees.

- Ganesha rides a **Mouse**. A mouse is compared to ego. An ego, like a mouse, nibbles humility and goodness from human beings. A mouse sitting near the feet of Ganesha indicates that a faultless person is the one who has conquered his or her ego.

- Some say Ganesha has two strengths – one is **Siddhi** and the second is **Riddhi**. Siddhi represents success and prosperity. Riddhi represents wisdom.

Saraswati

Saraswati is Brahma's wife. She is called the **Goddess of Knowledge**. Since knowledge is necessary for creation, Saraswati is considered to be the creative power of Lord Brahma.

Goddess Saraswati is shown wearing pure white clothes, seated on a white lotus. White means purity. Saraswati has four hands. In one hand she holds a book and in the other a rosary. With her other two hands, she is seen playing a musical instrument called the *veena*. Her vehicle is the swan. The festival of **Basant Panchmi** is dedicated to Goddess Saraswati.

Saraswati represents learning and wisdom and is the protector of all Vedic knowledge. Her presence on earth is manifested by the **river Saraswati** The Saraswati river flows from the Himalayas into the Indian Ocean. Saraswati, is the first river, which was granted the status of a Vedic Goddess. When the Aryans came from central Asia, they settled at the banks of the river Saraswati. Her soil was so fertile that the Aryans gave up their wandering existence and settled to a life of farming here! The river's soothing flow inspired sages and poets to meditate on her banks.

Aryan settlement at the banks of Saraswati river

Lakshmi

When the Gods churned the oceans, there was a moment when proceedings had to be stopped, because the mountain, by which they were churning, was slipping. Vishnu took the *avatar* of a tortoise and dived under, to support the mountain. Deep down the ocean, Vishnu, as **Kurma**, the tortoise, saw **Lakshmi**. his gaze was struck by her beauty. After he finished his tasks, Vishnu carried Lakshmi to the surface. He married her and made her his consort. She came to be known as Goddess Lakshmi thereon.

Kurma smitten by Lakshmi

Goddess Lakshmi is associated with prosperity and fortune. Lakshmi's birth from the ocean has given her unlimited fertility. On earth, she is also known as '*prakriti* ' or nature.

Lakshmi is portrayed in a female form with four arms. She is always busy distributing wealth and prosperity to the devotees. The lotus seat, which Lakshmi is sitting upon, signifies that while living in this world, one should enjoy its wealth, but not become obsessed with it.

Goddess Lakshmi

Each time Vishnu descended on earth in an *avatar*, he would marry an *avatar* of Lakshmi. When Vishnu appeared as **Parashurama**, he married Lakshmi as **Dharini**. When he was **Ram**, Lakshmi was born as **Sita**. As **Krishna**, Lord Vishnu married her as **Rukmini**.

Goddess Lakshmi is regularly worshipped in shrines at home and in temples by her devotees. A special worship is offered to her annually on **Diwali**.

Parashurama & Dharini

Ram & Sita

Krishna & Rukmini

Sati

Sati is also called **Uma**. She is the first wife of Shiva. The name Sati means a *true or virtuous woman*. On being insulted by her father, who was saying terrible things about her husband, Shiva, Sati sacrificed herself, by jumping into a blazing fire.

Shiva, hearing about the death of his wife, went mad with grief. Brahma and Vishnu were very upset to see this. Vishnu promised Shiva that he would get her back in another form. Not long after this, Sati was born as **Parvati**, the daughter of the Mountain King, **Himavat**.

Sati jumps into the fire

Parvati

As a child, Parvati was constantly lost in the worship of Shiva. When she finally married Shiva, Parvati knew her heartfelt wish had been granted. For Shiva too, it was an occasion to rejoice! Parvati, after all, was the reincarnation of his wife, Sati.

Parvati, presents two main facets to her worshippers: a gentle personality and a dangerous personality. In the form of Parvati, she is known as the spouse of Lord Shiva and is the mother of her two sons. In her other form she is called the destroyer of demons!

Parvati

Durga

Parvati as Shiva's wife is shown to be an ordinary housewife and a mother. However, there is another form Parvati takes. That is of **Durga**. As Durga, she becomes a *powerful warrior*. From this form of Durga, she takes many other forms for the destruction of demons who are troubling Gods and mankind. How did she get the name Durga?

Legends say that a Demon named **Mahishasura** (also called **Durg**), prayed hard to Lord Shiva for boons. Lord Shiva, impressed with his devotion, blessed him saying, "No man or deity would be able to kill you. You can only be killed by a woman."

Mahishasura was very pleased with this boon, as he thought that a woman can never defeat him. He grew so mighty that he conquered the three worlds. The displaced Gods begged Shiva for help. Shiva, being the all knowing deity, turned to his wife Parvati.

He appealed, "My wife, in you there is enormous strength. Draw from that and vanquish Mahishasura."

Durga killing Mahishasura

Parvati nodded. With a chant, she created **Kalaratri**, an extremely comely and beautiful female. Kalaratri's beauty was meant to bewitch the demon and trick him into restoring normality. The plan failed. Mahishasura sent soldiers to kill her. Kalaratri was unfazed. With a blow of air from her cheeks, she reduced the huddle of attacking soldiers to ashes! Not affected at all, Durg or Mahishasura then sent horrid looking demons to catch Kalaratri! The monsters frightened her so much that she fled to Parvati. Parvati immediately fell into a fierce battle with Durg. She changed many forms to battle every situation thrown at her by Durg. Durg used many weapons, took the image of an elephant and then a buffalo, but Parvati crushed him, along with his army, effortlessly.

Parvati was given the name Durga, *because she killed Durg*, better known as Mahishasura. She is worshiped during an annual festival called **Durga Puja**, especially popular among Bengalis.

Manifestations of Parvati…

Durga: In Sanskrit, it means 'she who is incomprehensible'. Durga is also called by many other names, such as *Parvati*, *Ambika*, and *Kali*. Her image is represented with ten arms; in one hand she holds a spear, with one of her left hands she holds the tail of a serpent, with another the hair of the giant whose breast the snake is biting; her other hands are filled with various weapons. She rides a lion.

Durga

Dasabhuja: This means the ten-handed one. She destroyed the demon army.

Singhavahini: The one with lion as the vehicle. Riding a lion; she fought with the army of **Chanda** and **Munda**, and has four arms only. She drank the blood of the *leaders*, and devoured a large part of their troops. As Singhavahini, she carries a sword and spear in two hands, and with two other hands is encouraging her devotees.

Mahishasurmardini: The slayer of Mahishasura.

Jagaddhatri: This means 'the mother of the world'. She is dressed in red garments and is seated on a lion. As Jagaddhatri, she carries a conch-shell, discus, bow and arrow.

Muktakesi: The one with flowing hair. This form destroyed another part of Durg's forces.

Singhavahini

Tara: She is called the Saviour. This form slewed one of the generals called **Sumbha** of the demon's army.

Chinnamastaka: In this form, she beheaded **Nisumbha**, the other demon.

Jagadgauri: The yellow Goddess who received the thanks and praises of the Gods and men for the deliverance she brought.

Pratyangira: In this form of Durga, no images are made, but at night, the officiating priest, wearing red clothes, offers red flowers, liquors and sacrifices to the Goddess.

Annapurna: She is the giver of food and is represented standing on a lotus, or as sitting on a throne. In one hand, she holds a rice bowl, and in the other, a spoon used for stirring rice.

Annapurna

Ganeshajanani: Mother of Ganesha; is worshipped with the infant Ganesha in her arms.

Ganeshajanani

Krishnakrora: When Krishna fought with the serpent Kaliya in the river Yamuna, he was bitten by the serpent, and while in pain, Krishna called upon Durga for help. She heard his cry, and by suckling him from her breast, restored him to health.

Krishnakrora

Kali

Kali is the form Parvati took to slew **Raktavija**, in order to help her son **Skanda** or **Kartekeya**.

She further took the image of **Chandi** in her form of Kali. The demon Raktavija had the powers to multiply himself whenever drops of his blood fell to the ground.

Kali

Kali or Chandi stretched her tongue and licked all the blood, before it touched the surface!

Kali is represented as a black goddess with four arms; in one hand she has a sword, in another the head of the giant she has slained. Her eyes are red as she stands with one foot on the thigh, and another on the breast of her husband.

It is said that after defeating the demons, Goddess Kali was overjoyed. She began to dance the dance of victory. Her dancing reached a furious peak and the earth trembled. The Gods were frightened. Shiva called out to Kali to stop.

Kali's Dance

But she did not hear him, since she was so lost in her celebratory dance. Shiva then lay down near her feet. She continued dancing until she caught sight of her husband under her feet, and then immediately thrust out her tongue with shame at the disrespect she had shown him and stopped.

Kali steps on Shiva

Ganga

Ganga is a *river Goddess*. She is one of India's seven sacred rivers. (**Gangotri** is from where she flows into the city of Hardiwar; Allahabad, where she joins the Yamuna; Varanasi, the holy city; and Sagara Island in her estuary, then she finally flows into the Bay of Bengal.)

Ganga, the pure and untainted Goddess, is the daughter of **Himavat** and **Mena**. She is Parvati's older sister. Mythology says that in a human form, Ganga married King **Shantanu** and was the mother of **Bhishma**, patron to the warring Pandava and Kaurava clans.

Ganga

Shiva traps Ganga in his hair

At first, Ganga was a river in the heavens. But King **Bhagiratha** obtained a boon from Brahma to allow Ganga to come down to earth. He needed Ganga to flow on earth to wash away the sins of his ancestors with her pure waters. Alas! Earth was so young that the impact of Ganga's fall and could disintegrate it. It was here that Shiva, after Bhagiratha requested him, agreed to stall the impact by allowing her to descend on his head. Shiva caught her in the coils of his hair and held her fast. In one of her seven streams, Ganga followed Bhagiratha and flowed over the ashes of his ancestors, to wash away their sins.

It is believed that where ever Ganga flows that place becomes sacred.

Gayatri

Gayatri is another consort of Lord Brahma. Gayatri's image has five heads. The four heads of Gayatri represent the four Vedas and the fifth head represents the Almighty God. She is seated on a lotus, swan or a peacock. She is wearing crowns on all five heads; the crowns bear nine types of gems, which signify Divine Light.

Radha

Radha is Krishna's devoted companion. As a Goddess she follows him wherever he takes her, trusting him completely and giving up her ego.

Radha and Krishna are
worshipped together
at temples

Radha and Krishna

Sita

Sita is said to have emerged at birth from the furrow of a ploughed field. Sita is supposed to be a reincarnation of Lakshmi, Lord Vishnu's wife. On earth, Sita is Ram's wife.

Born from mother earth, Sita has life-giving, fertile qualities and is shown as an ideal wife who represents wifely devotion to the fullest.

Ram and Sita

Minor Gods

Legends, tales, unforgettable acts of heroism, chart a strong route in the annals of Hindu mythology. Champions of stories were capable of such bravery that they were elevated to the status of Minor Gods.

The Minor Gods of Hinduism are...

Kamadeva

Kamadeva: He is the **God of love**. Kamdeva shoots with his bow, the five flower-tipped arrows of igniting love and desire.

Kubera: He is the **God of Wealth**. Kubera is the guardian of the North, watching over the earth's mineral wealth of gold, silver, jewels, pearls etc.

Kubera

Yakshas: They are the **attendants of Kubera**, the God of wealth, employed to guard his gardens and treasure.

Yakshas

Soma

Soma: He is the **Moon God** also known as Chandra.

Vishwakarma

Vishwakarma: The **Divine Architect** of the whole universe.

Yama

Yama: The **God of Death** and is the Lord of the infernal regions visited by man after cessation of life. He is the embodiment of the law of *karma* and imparts justice according to deeds.

Gandharvas

Gandharvas: are the **celestial musicians** who play in the court of Indra.

Kinnaras

Kinnaras: Mythical beings, with a body of a man and head of a horse. They are **singers** at the court of Indra.

Siddhas: Classes of spirits of great purity and holiness, who dwell alone in the sky or mid air between the earth and the heavens.

Manu: Created by Brahma, Manu means **'the man'.** This name also belongs to fourteen mythological characters of mankind.

Nachiketa: By his humility, **Nachiketa** won over the heart of Yama, the God of death and learnt the secrets of spiritual life from him.

Prahlad: Son of the demon-king **Hiranyakashipu**, he faced the anger of his mighty father for the sake of his faith in Lord Vishnu.

Prahlad

Bali: He was a devotee of Lord Vishnu. Though a king of demons, he ruled with righteousness and always had the welfare of his subjects at heart.

Dhruva: The grandson of Manu. His unflinching devotion to Vishnu raised him to the skies as the Pole Star.

Dhruva

Eklavya

Eklavya: He won the status of a Minor God when he smilingly sacrificed his thumb at the asking of his guru.

Harishchandra: He sacrificed everything he had at the altar of truth, including his kingdom and even his son.

Harishchandra

Did you Know?

- When sage Vyasa wanted to compose the **Mahabharata**, Brahma suggested Ganesha to be his scribe. Vyasa agreed and Ganesha used his broken tusk as a writing quill. Vyasa dictated the entire epic in verse and Ganesha recorded every word.

Ganesha writing the Mahabharata

- A day in Brahma's life measures four billion human years and is called a **Kalpa**.

- Goddess Lakshmi, Vishnu's wife, personifies not only substance possessions, but the richness of bravery, children, success, food, luxurious life and eternal bliss.

- The water of Ganga is graced with extraordinary properties of purification and does not putrefy even after years of being kept in bottles and jars. It is believed that even hardened criminals and sinners will go to heaven if they worship the Ganga.

Jagat Shri Brahma Temple

- **Jagat Shri Brahma Temple** is the only standing temple in India, dedicated to Lord Brahma. It is in Pushkar in Rajasthan. There are hardly any temples for Lord Brahma. Why? Brahma was cursed by Shiva (when he lied) that no one would pray to him, (Brahma), henceforth.

Children Books By

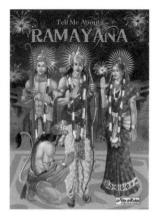

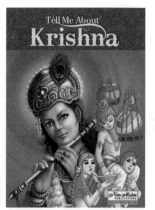

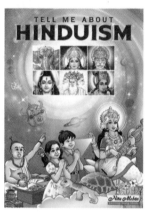

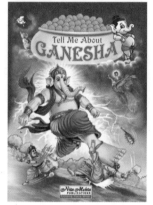

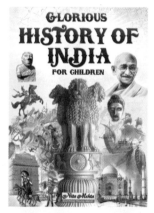

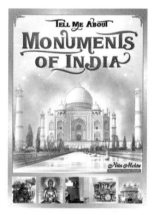

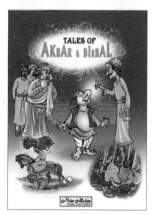

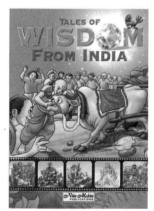

Children Books By

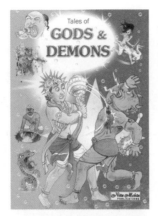
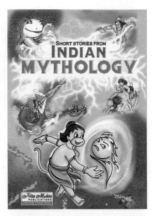